*Want more? Supplementary information, pictures and videos can be found at:*

sites.google.com/view/PastBroughtToLife

Second Edition published November 2020.

This book and the merged and contemporary photographs within are copyright © C.Partridge, 2020. All rights reserved.

The copyright of the "old" photographs is retained by the original owners. Every effort has been made to identify copyright holders and seek permission for their use in this booklet. If you believe copyrighted material has been used inadvertently please contact the author.

**Acknowledgements**

The author is grateful to those who provided photographs and information:
The Royal Pavilion and Museums, Brighton & Hove - brightonmuseums.org.uk
Regency Society – regencysociety.org
 and in particular the James Gray archive – regencysociety-jamesgray.com
The Sikh Museum www.sikhmuseum.com/brighton
Hove in the Past - hovehistory.blogspot.com
My Brighton & Hove - www.mybrightonandhove.org.uk
National Trust - www.nationaltrust.org.uk
East Brighton Bygones - www.bygones.org.uk
Fulking.net - www.fulking.net
Volks Electric Railway Association – volkselectricrailway.co.uk
The Roundhill Society - www.roundhill.org.uk
Simplon Postcards - www.simplonpc.co.uk
Private collections of Roy Wood, Brian Stothard, Geoffrey Wells, Peter Groves, and Margaret Stewart

# Contents

| | |
|---|---|
| Chain Pier | 3 |
| Fish Market | 4 |
| Bathing Machines | 5 |
| Thrale's House | 7 |
| Volk's Railways | 8 |
| Black Rock Lido | 14 |
| Trams | 15 |
| Preston Circus Fire Station | 19 |
| Devil's Dyke | 21 |
| First World War | 27 |
| Open Market | 29 |
| Graf Zeppelin | 30 |
| Second World War | 31 |
| Regent Cinema | 39 |
| Athina B | 40 |

# Chain Pier

Royal Pavilion & Museums, Brighton & Hove and C.Partridge

c1891 -1896

Built in 1823 Brighton's first pier was mainly intended as a landing stage for ships but it proved popular with visitors even with the steep 2d entrance fee. There were gift shops in some of the pylons and attractions were added later on the shore including a camera obscura, bazaar and lounge.

The Palace Pier was being built to replace it when a storm demolished the Chain Pier on the 4th December 1896. Its signal cannon is now on the Palace Pier along with its two entrance kiosks which serve as small shops (look for the octagonal booths with fish scale roofs just before the first arcade).

# Fish Market

Regency Society & C.Partridge                                                                                                                c1880

The area to the west of the Palace Pier was where the fishing industry was most concentrated, all the more so having been ejected from the town centre as it gentrified. A fish market operated on the beach before moving to a purpose built space in the arches from 1867 until 1960.

In the old image note the fishing nets hanging out to dry on the railings and the Gents bathing machines competing for space with the fishing boats on the crowded shore. The strange huts, bottom centre, house ropes and nets. The two rusty winches in the new image belong to Brighton Fishing Museum, but in the 1880s horse powered capstans would have hauled boats up the beach.

# Bathing Machines

Regency Society & C.Partridge                                                    c1900

Bathing machines were used for changing modestly. They had a door at both ends and clothes were stored on shelves inside. They would be pushed to the water's edge until the bather had finished then pulled back up the beach, normally by horse.

This area beside the West Pier was for ladies and children only.

Mixed bathing was finally permitted in 1901.

Royal Pavilion & Museums, Brighton & Hove & C.Partridge

21 September 1908

This photo was taken from the Palace Pier looking east. Note the cables used to winch boats and bathing machines up the beach.

Few knew how to swim in the 18th century so women used to be assisted by strong female "dippers" and men by male "bathers". Martha Gunn and John "Smoaker" Miles were the most famous, friends of royalty and first choice of celebrities. By the time this photo was taken the dippers were long gone but in rough seas a rope could be attached to the bathing machines for bathers to cling on to.

# Thrale's house

Royal Pavilion & Museums, Brighton & Hove & C.Partridge                                                                                                        Between 1865 - 1867

Here at the coastal end of West Street the building on the left of the old photo shows Brighton Arcade signage, but prior to that it was the fashionable family home of Henry & Hester Thrale from 1767. Samuel Johnson frequently visited the Thrales even though Hester reported he was no fan of Brighton saying it was *"so truly desolate… that if one had a mind to hang one's self for desperation at being obliged to live there, it would be difficult to find a tree on which to fasten the rope"*.

The Thrale's house featured a chain linked fence in front and you can see the 7 posts in this picture. While the buildings have changed completely one of the 250 year old posts remains to this day.

# Volk's Railways

Roy Wood, East Brighton Bygones & C.Partridge                                                        1895

When Magnus Volk first opened his electric railway in 1883 the line started more usefully at the Palace Pier but he was forced to shorten it in 1929 due to road widening and plans to build a swimming pool, though eventually the pool was built at Black Rock instead (see page 14).

Storms occasionally damaged the track, attached at this point to the outside of the sea wall. A wave can be seen spraying water over the line and drivers wore oilskins. Despite this cars ran every 6 minutes even in winter.

This image shows how the railway had to dip under the Chain Pier entrance. The dip was often wet and could cause electrical problems forcing the installation of an insulated third rail in 1886.

The shore side attractions mentioned on the Chain Pier page (p.3) can be seen here. The small tower perched on top was a camera obscura. The pier's suspension cables pass right through the buildings to the wall where they were anchored.

Regency Society

A tunnel exists on the same spot today, but reversed. Now Volk's railway goes over the top and pedestrians pass underneath to reach the beach.

Still running today Volk's creation is the world's oldest operating electric railway

Illustrated London News & C.Partridge

5 December 1896

When first built Volk's railway ended at Banjo groyne, which is opposite Paston Place. Volk wished to continue all the way to Rottingdean but the terrain made it impossible for a conventional line so he came up with this extraordinary invention to continue the journey.

Nicknamed the "Daddy Longlegs" the electric powered vehicle could travel in deep water. As it operated at sea maritime regulations applied requiring a trained sea captain be in charge and that it carry a life boat and lifebelts.

The Royal Pavilion and Museums, Brighton & Hove and C.Partridge 1900+

The unwieldy official title was "Brighton and Rottingdean Seashore Electric Railway", and the car itself was named "Pioneer".

Just days after opening on the 4th December 1896 the same storm that destroyed the chain pier (p.3) knocked over the moored Pioneer. However after a huge effort it was working again by July 1897.

Passengers could go outside on two levels or sit in some luxury inside and enjoy refreshments.

At low tide it could manage 6mph but slowed to less than walking speed at high tide. An engine upgrade was needed but was never profitable enough to justify it.

Power flowed in from an overhead line but the return current went through the sea. Best not swim too close!

It closed just 5 years later when the council built new groynes through the track.

Regency Society 1900

Simplon Postcards & C.Partridge

To partly compensate Volk for ending his sea railway he was allowed to extend his conventional electric railway to Black Rock, which he did in 1901. The original Paston Place terminus is now the Half Way station.

To extend the railway he simply ran the track out of the back of his train sheds. However this meant adding a small section of exposed track until it could gain the support of the sea wall. Unlike the wooden beams elsewhere this was made of steel.

Roy Wood via East Brighton Bygones & C.Partridge

The triangular area formed by the 1901 rail extension has since been concreted over and become an unsightly storage and waste area.

In all these seafront photos notice how low the beach was compared to today and how much nearer the sea. The natural eastward drift of the shingle has been prevented by groynes and the building of the Marina. As a result the beach continues to grow ever larger and the sea more distant.

# Black Rock Lido

Royal Pavilion & Museums, Brighton & Hove and C.Partridge

This open air saltwater pool operated between 1936 and 1978.

Volk's railway had already been shortened at the Palace Pier (see page 8) and the same happened at the Black Rock end to make way for the pool, shrinking the total line length from 1.25 to 1.05 miles.

When the Marina was built it did not replace the lido as some believe. Instead the site of the old lido lies derelict despite many plans to regenerate it.

# Trams

Regency Society & C.Partridge

1901

Tram tracks being laid in Marlborough Place, next to Victoria Gardens in 1901. The gardens were strictly reserved for residents until 1896, hence the tall railings which remained until the 1920s.

A farmhouse here was re-fronted in 1779 in Georgian style becoming the King & Queen pub. A hatch in the back wall secretly served soldiers from the barracks behind.

It changed into its current fanciful Mock Tudor form in 1939 though even its admirers described it as a "pantomime". The King and Queen referred to in its name were changed to Tudors (previously King George III and Queen Charlotte) but the serving hatch was preserved and is still visible today. Parts of both the old and new versions of the building are shown here.

Regency Society & C.Partridge

1902

Electric trams had just started running when this extension was built over Preston Circus. A brewery was demolished the previous year making space for these new lines, the Duke of Yorks cinema and a fire station.

The Hare & Hounds pub only claims to have been founded in 1905 but has actually occupied this spot since the early 19th century. However it was rebuilt in 1905, taking over "The Fox" next door.

Robert Bovington? & C.Partridge

A tram near the bottom of Elm Grove and the junction with the Lewes Road.

The 8 routes that made up the electric tram network were all built between 1901 and 1904. They remained in use until 1939.

The tram depot was on the Lewes Road. It still exists and is now used by the buses that replaced them. The windows there remain etched with "Brighton Corporation Tramways".

Roy Wood via East Brighton Bygones & C.Partridge

Trams and a trolleybus at Old Steine. The trolleybus was like a modern bus but still used the overhead electricity supply.

The last tram ran on 1st September 1939 and it was thought they were all turned into scrap for the war effort. However one was recently found on a pig farm and enthusiasts are endeavouring to restore it. See www.brightontram53.org.uk

# Preston Circus Fire Station

Regency Society & C.Partridge

1907

Brighton's first motorised fire engine sets off and a horse drawn version looks set to follow.

For a long time Brighton had a fragmented and not always effective fire service run by insurance companies and volunteers. By the time the original photo was taken the police had taken over the leading role and built this HQ in 1901, though volunteer brigades continued until 1921 when a single service took over everything. In 1938 the modern fire station was built here with its swept back frontage.

Regency Society & C.Partridge                                                                                                           1904

A horse drawn fire engine charges up the London Road on the wrong side, though as the main fire station lies just ahead at Preston Circus they are more likely racing home for tea than putting out a fire.

All the buildings in the street have changed except one which allows the exact location to be determined. The white, recessed house at number 87 used to be the Vicarage for nearby St Bartholomew's church.

# Devil's Dyke

Regency Society & C.Partridge

An outing to Devil's Dyke from Brighton would take over an hour each way by horse and wagonette, so the railway was immediately popular when it opened on the 1st September 1887 and ran for 51 years until the motor car took away its trade.

It terminated at what is now Dyke Farm as the gradient beyond was too steep leaving visitors to walk the last few hundred yards. Today much of the route is still easy to identify and some platform remnants and fencing can still be found.

Regency Society & C.Partridge

Between 1894-1908

The increased visitor numbers inspired James Henry Hubbard to buy the Dyke estate in 1892 and he set about building it into a major attraction, peaking at 30,000 visitors on Whit Monday 1893.

Attractions Hubbard built at Devil's Dyke included a fun fair, monorail bicycles, a switchback railway (an early roller coaster) and even a giant wooden gun along with this dramatic cable car.

An existing refreshment hut built in 1817 was extended to become the Inn shown above.

The cable car had many names, one of the most common being the "aerial cableway".

Intrepid Victorian passengers would pass through gaps in the pylons and across the Dyke, suspended in a small cage up to 230 feet above the ground.

It is believed to be the first passenger carrying cable car in the UK.

Today concrete blocks can still be found on both sides of the dyke revealing the locations of the pylons.

Regency Society & C.Partridge

Between 1894-1908

The aerial cableway shown from another angle.

It took 2 minutes and 15 seconds to travel between the two small station huts, a distance of 1,100 feet.

It opened in 1894 and closed around 1908 or 1909.

About 150 yards north east of the modern day Devil's Dyke pub a funicular railway ran up the northern face of the Downs.

Unusually the gradient varied over the length of the track. That meant the up and down cars did not balance each other out and more demands were made on the engine. The cars moved at a leisurely 3mph.

It had a relatively short life running from 1897 to 1908.

Regency Society & C.Partridge                    c1900

The engine room foundations are still visible, as is a long indentation indicating where the tracks ran, though they now descend into a forest.

This photograph shows the building remnants. The village of Poynings can also be seen below. Tea rooms quickly opened there for visitors.

Financially the funicular was a mistake. Not only was it unprofitable it also encouraged visitors to spend money down in Poynings instead of the Dyke.

Regency Society and C.Partridge

The bottom of the funicular connected to a footpath. Most travellers turned right towards the Poynings tea rooms and the Royal Oak, however they could also choose to turn left and use this footpath to visit Fulking.

# First World War

Regency Society & C.Partridge

21 August 1915

These soldiers, led by bandsmen, have marched to Seven Dials and turned down Buckingham Place towards the station on their way to fight in the First World War.

Royal Pavilion & Museums, Brighton & Hove and C.Partridge                                                                                                              1915

12,000 injured Indian troops were treated in Brighton during WW1. The best known location was the Royal Pavilion but there were many more. The smallest were private houses and the largest a converted workhouse on Elm Grove renamed the Kitchener Indian Hospital (now Brighton General).

The town was fascinated by the exotic troops. At the Kitchener, Col. Bruce Seton feared the interest of local women might result in "scandals" so in 1915 he added barbed wire, a police cordon and threatened floggings should any patient try to leave. The prison atmosphere caused so much tension an Indian orderly shot at the colonel with a revolver, but missed. After that restrictions were eased.

# Open Market

Regency Society & C.Partridge

c1919

"Barrow Boys" started selling fruit and vegetables in Brighton in the 1890s but it really took off when servicemen returning from the first world war were unable to find employment and joined them.

Oxford Street was one key location but local shops complained so in the 1920s (around the time of this photograph) the council tried to remove them resulting in the "Battle of Oxford Street". Barrow Boys blocked the London Road until truncheon wielding police finally managed to clear it, but the council got the message and granted the Open Market new sites. Today it has a purpose built home.

## *Graf Zeppelin*

30

Brian Stothard via My Brighton & Hove

31 August 1931

The Graf Zeppelin was enormous, the largest ever airship at the time it was built in 1928. It was the first airship to circumnavigate the world and in total it covered over a million miles before being retired after the Hindenburg disaster.

On 31 August 1931 it flew over Brighton and Eastbourne. It is shown here behind what was Avery's shop near the top of the St James' street.

# Second World War

Royal Pavilion & Museums, Brighton & Hove and C.Partridge

Early September 1939

Madeira Drive looking towards the Albion Hotel. During the war the Aquarium (now called the Sea Life Centre) was requisitioned by the R.A.F. along with many of the larger hotels. Here we see it being extensively fortified with sandbags.

Royal Pavilion & Museums, Brighton & Hove and C.Partridge

1-2 September 1939

Even before the Second World War was officially declared evacuee children started arriving at Brighton Station from London to escape the bombs, and that was true nationally. Almost all the 1½ million children who were evacuated reached their reception areas by the 3rd September 1939 when war was declared.

However in 1940 as the threat of invasion grew some of Brighton's own children were evacuated elsewhere.

Royal Pavilion & Museums, Brighton & Hove and C.Partridge                                                                                             1944

Brighton has not always welcomed foreign visitors. Following the fall of France in June 1940 the British coastal towns looked vulnerable. Brighton's beaches were closed and fortified.

Here beside the Palace Pier are anti-tank concrete blocks and barbed wire. Gaps were knocked in both piers to impede their use during an invasion, booby traps were installed, pillboxes built and the beach was mined.

Councillor Geoffrey Wells via My Brighton & Hove & C.Partridge    c1900

The Lewes Road Inn opened in 1864 and this picture was taken around 1900.

Notice the wall behind the beer barrels lines up with the building beside it and compare that with the next image.

Peter Groves via My Brighton & Hove & C.Partridge

September 1940

The building was completely destroyed when it was bombed on the 20th Sept 1940. Several staff were killed but the barmaid and pub dog were rescued from the rubble.

The modern part of the image shows the rebuilt pub wall has retreated from the road, but it expanded to take over Stokes & Son coal merchant next door leaving it a similar size inside. After a spell as the Franklin Tavern it has now reverted to its original name, The Lewes Road Inn.

Margaret Stewart & C.Partridge

March 1943

Gunner Bruno Anderson of the Royal Canadian Artillery and his anti-aircraft Bofors gun & crew outside the Grand Hotel. Many of Brighton's defences were manned by Canadian troops.

A sign on the lamp post indicates the nearest air raid shelter.

Rumour has it the Bofors gun crews had orders to destroy the piers in the event of an invasion.

37

Royal Pavilion & Museums, Brighton & Hove and C.Partridge                                       2nd December 1944

On 26th November 1944 four Typhoons took off from Eindhoven in Holland to escort Air Marshal Breadner to Britain. One got into trouble and pilot F/Lt John Brown crash landed in front of Embassy Court.

The pilot was injured but survived.

Royal Pavilion & Museums, Brighton & Hove and C.Partridgec1945

With the ending of the war in Europe the sea mines needed clearing.

This one is being made safe near the Palace Pier by members of HMS Vernon, a torpedo and mine training facility based at Roedean Girls School. They relocated there from Portsmouth in 1941 after being heavily bombed.

# Regent Cinema

Royal Pavilion & Museums, Brighton & Hove and C.Partridge

July 1930

The ornate Regent Cinema 1921 – 1973, located on Queens Road near the clock tower. It could seat 3,000 and also featured a large ballroom with a sprung floor.

An Austin Whippet has been suspended outside to promote an early talkie film "Hell's Angels". The aircraft was tiny, British and designed for leisure. It was certainly not a German fighter as it is pretending to be here! Only 5 were ever made.

The site is now part of Boots.

# Athina B

Royal Pavilion & Museums, Brighton & Hove, Lavender Jones and C.Partridge

January 1980

The Athina B was carrying a cargo of pumice stone destined for Shoreham harbour when her engines failed. The crew were rescued in stormy weather leaving the ship to drift. The next day on 21st January 1980 it ran aground on Brighton beach.

The ship's anchor can be found on a plinth in Madeira Drive.

Printed in Great Britain
by Amazon